Plants! How They Change with the Seasons

(Botany for Kids)

Children's Botany Books

Left Brain Kids

Educational Books for Children

Kids, what is your favorite season of the year? How do plants respond to the seasons?

Winter, spring, summer and fall…

Plants in the spring!

Since it is usually rainy in the spring, people start planting. The days are getting longer and warmer.

It is the time for change for plants. The seeds sprout. This is called germination. Likewise, the buds on trees and shrubs open into leaves and flowers.

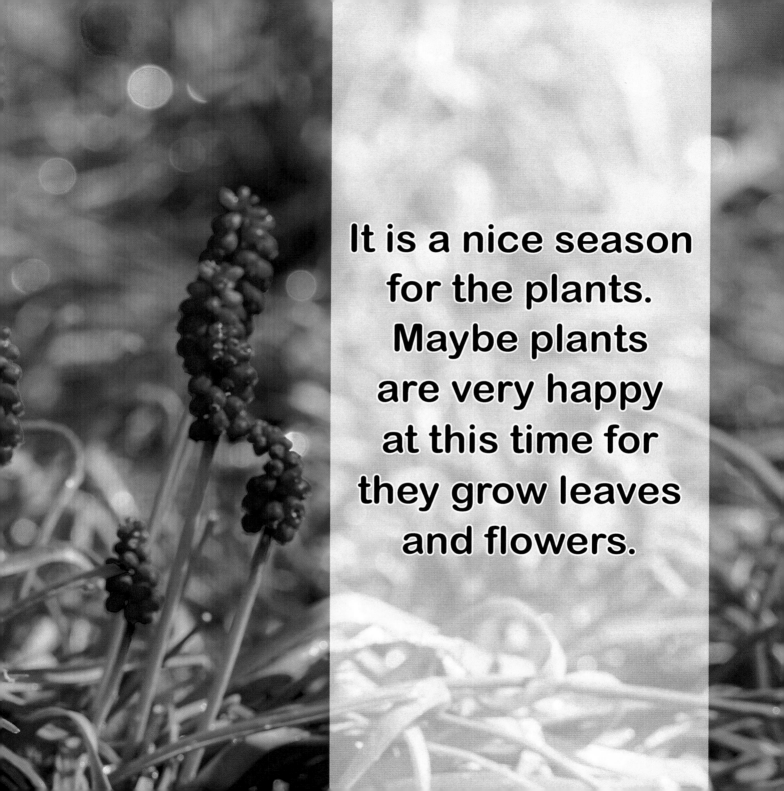

It is a nice season for the plants. Maybe plants are very happy at this time for they grow leaves and flowers.

Plants in the summer!

In this season many plants grow flowers and fruit. Summer days are the longest days.

It means there is plenty of sunlight. The plants are very happy! Plants are at their tallest height at this time.

Fruit is also growing, but some is not ripe. Trees and other plants are thick with leaves.

Plants
in fall!

The leaves of many trees change their color and fall off. The sunlight is less and the days are shorter.

Trees respond
by dropping
their fruit as
it gets ripe!

Many fruits and vegetables are ready for harvest. It's the harvest season!

Plants in the winter days!

Some places have experienced scarcity of food. Frost forms over the plants, seeds and roots.

Many plants lose their leaves. Trees have no fruits. Most plants slow down and sleep for the winter, but some do not survive until spring.

Just like the plants and other living beings, we tend to adjust to changing warmth, length of day, and the changes of the season.

We should celebrate the seasons all around the year! Nature forms its wonders with the seasons!

Made in United States
North Haven, CT
08 December 2023

45395634R00024